HOLY SHIFT

For People Who Love Jesus…
but Cuss A Little. A Lot.

Buz Deliere

Deliere Media

Copyright © 2026 Deliere Media

All rights reserved.

No part of this publication may be reproduced, distributed, or transmitted in any form or by any means—electronic, mechanical, photocopying, recording, or otherwise—without the prior written permission of the author, except in the case of brief quotations used in articles or reviews.

For permission requests, contact:
Deliere Media askme@buzdeliere.com
Or visit: buzdeliere.com

Holy Shift: For People Who Love Jesus… but Cuss A Little. A Lot.

Cover design by: Buz Deliere

Printed in the United States of America

Scripture quotations are taken from the Christian Standard Bible®, Copyright © 2017 by Holman Bible Publishers. Used by permission. All rights reserved.

This book is a work of creative nonfiction. Some names and identifying details may have been changed to protect privacy. The opinions and experiences expressed are the author's own.

*To the ones who taught me how to speak,
and the ones who taught me how to listen.*

*To every coach, cook, coworker, and choir grandma
who ever side-eyed me mid-sentence, thanks for the grace.*

*To the readers walking this same wild road:
you're not alone, you're not too late, and you're not doing it wrong.
Thanks for showing up.*

*And to Jesus,
for saving not just my soul,
but also my sense of humor.*

*This one's for all of us who love God…
And who are still working on how we talk.*

CONTENTS

Title Page

Copyright

Dedication

Before We Begin... Let's Talk About Swearing.

Introduction: This Isn't About Being Perfect — It's About Being Honest

Chapter One: In the Beginning Was the Word... and That Word Was $#@!	1
Reflection	20
Chapter Two: What the Bible Actually Says (And What It Doesn't)	22
Reflection	35
Chapter Three: The Dangit Dilemma: Why Clean Words Feel So Weird (At First)	37
Reflection	44
Chapter Four: How to Catch It Before You Shout It	46
Reflection	51
Chapter Five: Alphabetical Outbursts (That Won't Get You Kicked Out of Bible Study)	53
Reflection	64

Chapter Six: What to Say When You Drop a Pan, Miss a Turn, or Slam a Finger	66
Reflection	71
Chapter Seven: Grace for the Slip-Ups	73
Reflection	78
Chapter Eight: Raising Kids and Talking Clean at Home	80
Reflection	85
Chapter Nine: How to Be Clean Without Being Cringe	87
Reflection:	93
Chapter Ten: Because Growth Doesn't Always Sound Polished	95
Reflection:	99
A Note From the Author	100
Final Prayer	101
The Holy Shift Field Manual (Quick Recap Edition)	102
Acknowledgement	105

BEFORE WE BEGIN... LET'S TALK ABOUT SWEARING.

I didn't grow up in a monastery. I didn't graduate from Bible college. I didn't always say "bless it" when I stubbed my toe. In fact, for most of my life, swearing was just... normal. I worked in kitchens, played sports, lived life with the volume turned all the way up, and when life got loud, so did my language. Then something shifted. I found Christ later in life, and suddenly, I cared about things I used to shrug off. My heart changed... but my habits? Not so much. I didn't stop loving Jesus when I got cut off in traffic. I didn't stop believing in grace when I dropped a hot skillet on my foot. But my words didn't always reflect the new life I was trying to live.

I'll be real, I struggled. Not because I didn't love God, but because I didn't know how to speak differently without sounding fake, cheesy, or like I was trying way too hard. So I started experimenting. I paid attention to my triggers. I came up with clean (and sometimes hilarious) alternatives. I built a new vocabulary, one that honored my faith *and* still felt like me.

That's what this book is. It's not a list of rules. It's not about guilt or perfection.

It's a tool. A guide. A survival kit for people like us, who love Jesus… but cuss a little. So if you've ever yelled something unholy after stepping on a Lego…Or if your toddler left a Barbie on the stairs and your bare foot found it at 6 a.m…Or if you've ever muttered "crap snacks" in the preschool pickup line…You're in good company. Let's clean up our words, without losing our edge. Let's laugh, learn, lean on grace and let's make a Holy Shift.

INTRODUCTION: THIS ISN'T ABOUT BEING PERFECT — IT'S ABOUT BEING HONEST

I used to think swearing was just part of who I was. It came out naturally — in the kitchen during rush hour, on the field in the middle of a heated game, or when life decided to hit me with one of those "are you serious right now?" moments. I didn't plan it. I didn't think about it. The words just flew.

When I came to know Christ, a lot in my life shifted. Some things changed right away. The way I saw people, the things I cared about, the kind of peace I'd never had before. But one thing that didn't disappear overnight was my vocabulary. I still dropped the occasional F-bomb when I burned my hand or slammed a cabinet. I still had moments where my words didn't line up with my heart, and that left me feeling stuck between two worlds: the old me and the one I was becoming.

For a while, I honestly didn't know what to do with that tension. I didn't want to fake some squeaky-clean persona that didn't feel like me, but I also didn't want to keep talking like I hadn't changed at all. That's when I realized this wasn't just a behavior issue. It was a *pattern* — something wired into how I responded to stress, pain, frustration, and even humor. It wasn't just about the words. It was about what those words were doing in me, and what they were saying about what was still unfinished in my heart.

This book isn't about being the language police. It's not about judging people who curse or pretending like I've got it all figured out. It's about helping people like you and me recognize the patterns that lead to those words, and learning how to interrupt them with something better. It's about getting honest with ourselves without getting discouraged. And it's about building a new vocabulary that reflects our growth without making us sound like we're trying too hard.

You won't find perfection here. But you will find stories, strategies, Scripture, and maybe even a few laughs. I've spent the last several years working to clean up my speech — not out of guilt, but because I want my words to carry the same weight as my faith. And I've found that when we make space for better words, we also make space for a better witness.

This isn't a book just for pastors or polished believers. It's for the everyday Christian who loves Jesus but still struggles when the hammer hits the thumb instead of the nail. It's for the parent who's trying not to cuss in front of their kids. For the young believer wondering if it really matters. For the former sailor or the current chef who needs a few cleaner options in the heat of the moment.

If that's you, you're not alone. You're in the right place. Let's laugh a little, learn a lot, and take a few intentional steps together.

Let's make a *Holy Shift*.

CHAPTER ONE: IN THE BEGINNING WAS THE WORD... AND THAT WORD WAS $#@!

"I tell you that on the day of judgment people will have to account for every careless word they speak. For by your words you will be acquitted, and by your words you will be condemned." — Matthew 12:36-37

Part 1: My Story & The Psychology of Swearing

There's a unique kind of chaos that happens in a professional kitchen. It's not the slow, simmering kind. It's fast, fiery, and unpredictable, more like a hurricane being duct-taped to a pressure cooker. If you've never been on the line during a Friday night dinner rush, imagine juggling flaming swords while someone yells tickets at you in a foreign language and another person behind you spills boiling water on the floor. That's the environment where I learned to work. And also where I learned to cuss like a sailor.

At the time, it didn't feel wrong. Swearing wasn't something I thought about, it was just part of the job. Part of the world I lived in. You drop a hot pan? You swear. You burn a sauce? You swear. The server forgets to ring in a table's order and now you've got six steaks going out late? You let it fly. I wasn't trying to offend anyone. I was just surviving the heat, literally and figuratively.

Long before I was ever a believer, language was my release valve. I'd grown up around it, played sports with it, worked with it, even chased fugitives with it. (Yes, I was a bounty hunter for a while but we'll save *that* story for another time.) In every high-stress environment I found myself in, swearing was the background music. It added rhythm to the chaos. It was the emotional punctuation for everything from adrenaline to frustration to gallows humor.

If I'm being honest, it worked. At least, it worked in the moment. It made me feel heard. It helped me vent. It bonded me to my crew, to my teammates, to people who didn't need the situation sugarcoated. We spoke in hard-edged syllables that cut through the noise. We didn't hold back because holding back felt like weakness. Clean language was something you used in church, or maybe on a job interview. Not in the trenches. Not when things were burning down.

Then I found faith or more accurately, faith found me, and everything started to shift.

Why We Swear: Psychology, Pressure, and Pattern

Swearing isn't random. It's not just a "bad habit" we pick up for fun. There are deep psychological and neurological reasons why certain words come flying out of our mouths when life smacks us in the face.

At its core, swearing is a response to intensity — whether it's pain, anger, stress, or even joy. It's an emotional reflex that taps directly into the amygdala, the part of your brain responsible for fight-or-flight. You don't think about swearing, you *feel* it. You react with it. That's why even people who haven't sworn in years might suddenly blurt something out when they slam their hand in a door or narrowly avoid a car accident. The brain doesn't ask for permission, it just unloads.

Researchers have found that swearing actually *reduces pain* in the short term. One study from Keele University in the UK had participants submerge their hands in ice water. Those who were allowed to swear lasted significantly longer than those who used neutral language. Why? Because profanity triggers a small release of adrenaline, which increases pain tolerance. It literally makes you feel stronger, temporarily.

But here's the catch, the more often you swear, the *less effective* it becomes. What started as a natural pressure release becomes habitual. That's where the pattern forms. Over time, our brains hardwire certain phrases or exclamations to certain emotions. Frustration = F-bomb. Annoyance = S-word. Surprise = whatever your go-to is. It becomes the path of least resistance — the phrase that's been carved into the trails of your nervous system over years of repetition.

Think of your brain like a hiking trail. The more you walk a path, the more worn it becomes. Eventually, it's no longer a decision, it's muscle memory. You've created a *reflex response* without realizing it. That's why people say "it just slipped out." They're not lying. It really *did* just happen, because the habit took over before consciousness kicked in.

Now multiply that by decades. Add in pressure, heat, chaos, exhaustion. Add in years of jobs like kitchens, construction sites, sports teams, military, police, bounty hunting — environments where the culture doesn't just *allow* swearing, it practically demands it. That kind of repetition doesn't just disappear when you give your life to Christ. You don't suddenly get a new vocabulary overnight. That's not how transformation works. That's not how the brain works either.

Here's the hard truth, most of us *don't even realize* how often we swear until we try to stop.

The first time I really noticed was after I got serious about my faith. I wasn't trying to be perfect, I just wanted my language to reflect what was going on inside me. But the moment I tried to clean it up, I realized how deeply embedded it was. Not just the obvious words, the "big" ones, but the muttered sarcasm, the passive-aggressive tone, the frustration masked in humor. It was all still there. Still automatic.

That's when I realized this wasn't just about language.
It was about *wiring*, and if I wanted to change the output, I had to start rewiring the system.

"It's Just Words"... or Is It? Why Our Vocabulary Matters More Than We Think

We live in a world where language is treated like it's disposable. People say things without thinking. They post, rant, text, joke, and explode — all in real time — and expect the world to just absorb it. "Don't be so sensitive," they'll say. "It's just words." But deep down, we know that's not true.

Words start wars, words start marriages. Words ruin friendships, words raise children and words shape faith. Words have weight.

Scripture backs this up again and again. Proverbs 18:21 doesn't say, "The tongue is no big deal." It says, *"The tongue has the power of life and death."* That's not poetic fluff, that's straight fire from God. Our words are not neutral. They build or they break. They bless or they burn.

You already know this, whether you realize it or not. Think back to a time someone said something to you that stuck, not something physical, just a sentence. Maybe it was a coach who called you soft, a parent who said, "You'll never be anything," or a friend who lashed out in anger. Years later, you might not remember what you were wearing that day, but you remember *exactly* how those words felt.

Now flip that. Maybe someone once said, "I'm proud of you," or "You've got what it takes," or "God's hand is on your life," and those words lit something up inside you, something that kept burning when everything else around you got dark.

That's the power of words. So no, it's not *just* language. What we say matters. How we say it matters. And what we repeat, we eventually become. Jesus said it even more plainly: *"Out of the overflow of the heart, the mouth speaks."* (Luke 6:45) That one hits hard. Because it means our words aren't just slipping out, they're leaking out. They're spilling from whatever is stored inside. And if that doesn't mess with your head a little, it should.

That means our vocabulary, especially the stuff we say when we're angry, tired, or caught off guard — is a mirror of what's really going on beneath the surface. The way we speak under pressure reveals where we are in the process of becoming. This doesn't mean we're doomed every time we mess up. That's not the point. Grace is real, and God's not sitting there with a swear jar waiting to smack us every time we say something out of pocket. But if we want to *grow*, we've got to be willing to *notice*. To pay attention. To ask:
"Why did I just say that?"

"Where did that come from?"
"What's going on inside me that makes this word feel necessary?"

Those aren't guilt-trip questions. They're growth questions. They're the start of something deeper than just *editing your vocabulary.* They're the start of *rewriting your inner script.*

The Culture of Cussing: Where We Picked It Up and Why It Stuck

For most of us, swearing wasn't taught, it was absorbed.

We didn't sit down in third grade and get a crash course on creative cursing. No one gave us a workbook titled *How to Swear Like an Adult in Ten Easy Steps*. It just sort of happened. One moment we're saying "shoot" when we drop our juice box, and the next thing you know we're in high school letting four-letter words fly like punctuation in a Quentin Tarantino script.

Language is one of the most contagious things on earth. You don't just hear it, you *catch* it. And the more you're around it, the more normal it feels.

Growing up, I caught a whole lot of it. Not because I was a rebel or trying to be edgy, it was just how people talked. On the field, in the kitchen, in the locker room, at the shop. Swearing wasn't taboo, it was expected. If you didn't cuss, people assumed you were either new, uptight, or about to report them to HR.

In professional kitchens, especially, cursing is practically part of the training. I've heard people say that working on the line is like going into battle and while that may be a little dramatic, it's not far off. When tickets start piling up, the grill's smoking, the fryer's spitting, and someone just 86'd the special without telling you, the kitchen turns into a war zone of heat, knives, fire, and emotion. And the soundtrack? Swearing. Loud, fast, creative swearing.

To be honest, it's kind of an art form in those settings. I've heard combinations of words that would make a pirate blush and a poet take notes. It's not just the classics either, it's layered. You stub your toe in a kitchen, and the curse that comes out is a sentence, a sound effect, and a philosophy paper all rolled into one. People aren't just mad, they're performing.

It's not just kitchens. I've played competitive sports, worked construction, and yes, even tracked down fugitives as a bounty hunter. (Which, by the way, is the only job where it's socially acceptable to yell "Come out with your hands up!" before breakfast.) In all those worlds, swearing was part of the culture. It wasn't even rebellious, it was just *how people communicated.*

That's what makes it so hard to unlearn.

When something becomes part of the background noise in your life, you stop noticing it. Like the hum of a fridge or the buzz of fluorescent lights. You get used to it. You accept it. And after a while, you stop questioning whether it *should* be there.

So when we start walking with Christ and feel convicted to change our speech, we're not just fighting against words, we're pushing back against an entire culture we've lived in for years. We're trying to reprogram something that was never consciously installed in the first place. That's not easy. And it's not instant.

That's why it's important to approach this with grace. You're not weak because you still struggle with language. You're not unspiritual because you dropped something and said something. You're human. You're undoing years, maybe decades, of conditioning.

Here's why you don't have to worry, just like you caught bad habits, you can also catch *better* ones.

Unlike the flu, these kinds of things are worth catching.

Words as Armor: How Language Became Our Emotional Defense System

For a lot of us, swearing isn't just about expressing emotion, it's about *protecting* ourselves from it.

We don't just use strong words because things get heated. Sometimes, we use them to keep people from getting too close. Over time, we learn that language can be a kind of emotional armor. The more we've been hurt, challenged, or pushed around, the more we start to rely on that armor to survive.

Think about it: when someone's struggling to express grief or pain or fear, what do they usually do? They don't cry openly or admit they're scared, at least not in the environments I came from. No, they deflect. They blow up. They throw out a hard-edged sentence packed with expletives because it feels safer than saying, "I'm hurting."

That's not just a communication style, it's a defense mechanism, and I've lived it.

As a younger man, especially in competitive environments like football or bounty hunting, vulnerability wasn't just uncomfortable, it was dangerous. You didn't show weakness. You didn't let anyone see you rattled. So when pressure built, I didn't process emotions — I threw up a wall made of words. Harsh ones. Fast ones. Words that dared anyone to challenge me.

The irony is that the stronger those words sounded, the more they usually covered something weak.
I wasn't angry — I was disappointed.
I wasn't mad — I was hurt.
I wasn't tough — I was guarded.

Swearing gave me control. It made me feel like I still had the upper hand, even when life was kicking my teeth in. It became the quickest way to push back against chaos, and because I didn't have the tools or maturity to name what I was *actually* feeling, I defaulted to language that was loud, sharp, and familiar.

It's strange how we start to equate swearing with strength.

The more I grew in my faith, the more I realized that real strength isn't loud, it's *disciplined*. It's not in how fast you can snap back, but in how carefully you choose your words when your flesh is begging to unload. That kind of strength takes self-awareness, self-control, and a willingness to pause.

You don't have to swear to be real, and you don't have to be fake to speak with kindness.

Jesus was the most powerful communicator the world has ever known, and not once did He rely on profanity to make His point land. That doesn't mean He was soft. In fact, He spoke hard truths constantly but He did it with precision. With purpose. With power that came from peace, not panic.

When I think about the way I used to speak, especially when life wasn't going my way, I realize I wasn't just venting. I was shielding. I was using language to manage fear, disappointment, stress, and shame. The crazy part is, I didn't even know it. I thought I was just "expressing myself." Now I see that I was protecting myself, and there's a big difference between the two.

The moment I started to unpack that, the moment I recognized that certain words were acting like armor, I also started to see that maybe God was inviting me to take the armor off. Not to be exposed or humiliated, but to be *healed*. Healing can't happen through a wall, it happens in the open. In the honest. In the unfiltered moments when we let God into the places we've been guarding for years.

So no, cleaning up your language isn't just about swapping curse words for Christian catchphrases. It's about learning to stop hiding behind your mouth and start speaking from your *heart*.

That's where the real shift begins.

Part 2: Neural pathways, patterns, and spiritual growth

There's a funny thing that happens when you burn yourself in a kitchen, your body reacts faster than your brain. One second, you're grabbing a hot pan handle you *thought* was safe, and the next, your hand's in the sink and your mouth is halfway through a word that's probably not in the Psalms.

It happens in milliseconds. Before you even register the pain, something comes flying out of your mouth. That, my friend, is your nervous system on autopilot.

Most people think of habits as routines — brushing your teeth, locking the door, putting your seatbelt on. Habits run deeper than conscious routines. They live in the unconscious parts of your brain, and they're often formed in moments of *emotionally heightened repetition*.

Let me explain. When you experience something intense — pain, fear, embarrassment — your brain does you a favor. It creates a shortcut so that next time you don't have to think, you just *react*. This is helpful if you're dodging a punch, diving for cover, or avoiding a hot stove, but it's less helpful when your brain wires "emotional outburst" to "verbal explosion." The more frequently that response happens, the deeper the neural groove becomes, and before long, it's not even a decision. It's a *default*.

If you've ever cussed without even realizing it, that's why. If you've ever muttered a phrase your parents used to say, even though you swore you never would, that's why. Your brain is doing what it thinks is efficient. It's choosing the fastest route it knows to get from emotion to expression.

Now imagine how many times those pathways have been reinforced over decades of stress, work, family drama, relational tension, and daily frustrations. You're not dealing with a language issue, you're dealing with *neuroplasticity*, and the only way to change it... is to interrupt it.

Here's what that looks like:
You get triggered — by pain, stress, disrespect, spilled coffee, whatever — and your brain reaches for the familiar phrase. That word is right there on the tip of your tongue. Instead of letting it fly, you *catch it*. Even if it's just barely. You pause. You grit your teeth. You mutter something

different. Maybe it's awkward. Maybe it's silly. Maybe it's just a heavy exhale and a prayer under your breath. But you *interrupt* the pattern.

That one moment of interruption creates a fork in the road. Your brain now has to consider a new path, and every time you choose it, you strengthen it. Over time, those new choices become easier. Not because you're trying harder, but because you've trained a new reflex. You've formed a new groove in your brain that says, *"We don't say that anymore. We go this way now."* And yeah, it takes time.

I remember trying to swap out words in the middle of the kitchen rush. "Son of a—blessing!" doesn't roll off the tongue the same way. The first dozen times I tried to hold back, I sounded like someone short-circuiting mid-sentence. My team thought I was developing a stutter or speaking in tongues.

Slowly, and I mean *slowly*, those weird substitutions started to feel natural. Not polished. Not perfect. But *possible.* This is the part of the journey that nobody sees. The rewiring. The in-between stage where you're no longer comfortable cussing like before, but not yet fluent in your new vocabulary either. It's awkward, and humbling, and kind of hilarious.

That's the beauty of it, because you're not just learning new words, you're reclaiming your voice.

Language and Identity: Who Do You Want to Sound Like?

The words we choose say more about us than we realize.

You can tell a lot about someone by the way they speak — not just what they say, but how they say it. Their vocabulary, tone, timing, and even their go-to exclamations all form a kind of verbal fingerprint. Whether we like it or not, people use that fingerprint to figure out who we are.

This isn't about impressing people. It's about *influence*. If you've ever had someone say, "I didn't expect you to say that," after you let a word slip, you've felt it. That moment of tension between who you're trying to be and who you used to be. You may still feel like the same person inside, but your words are sending mixed messages. That's the power of language. It's not just communication, it's identity projection.

Now, here's the hard part for those of us who came to faith later in life, we often have two vocabularies. We've got our *old default*, the one we used in kitchens, locker rooms, stressful jobs, or heated arguments, and we've got our *new direction* — the version of us that's trying to walk in grace, patience, and peace. The version that doesn't want to lash out every time life gets hard, but when pressure hits, the old vocabulary usually shows up first. Not because we're hypocrites but because we're human. Because when identity is shifting, language is often the last thing to catch up.

This is why growth can feel so frustrating. You've changed your heart, you've shifted your mindset and you're doing the inner work, but one dropped coffee cup or stubbed toe and suddenly it's like your mouth didn't get the memo. But let me encourage you, the fact that you *notice* it now is a sign that God's already doing something in you. Before, you didn't blink. Now you feel the tension. That tension is called conviction and it's a gift. It's not shame, it's not failure, it's a signal from your soul that you're no longer okay with staying the same.

When I first started thinking about how I spoke, really thinking about it, I had to ask myself some hard questions:

- Who do I want to sound like when I'm under pressure?

- What kind of man do I want my kids, my friends, my crew to hear?

- Do my words reflect the kind of strength that builds or the kind that breaks?

Maybe the most important one:
Would someone be surprised to find out I'm a follower of Christ based on how I talk when things get hard?

That one stuck with me. Not because I want to walk around performing holiness like some Christian robot. That's not real and it's not the goal. The goal isn't to sound like someone else, it's to become the *best, truest version* of who God already sees in you. You don't have to sound like a preacher. You just need to sound like someone who's growing. Someone whose words are catching up with their calling. No, you won't always get it right, but every time you choose peace over panic, kindness over edge, or restraint over reaction, you're practicing the language of your new identity.

You're sounding more like the person you're becoming.

Clean Speech ≠ Weak Speech: Why Toning It Down Isn't Selling Out

Let's get one thing straight, speaking with self-control isn't weakness. In fact, it might be one of the strongest things you ever do.

Somewhere along the way, especially in tough environments — kitchens, construction sites, sports teams, law enforcement, even certain friend groups — swearing became a badge of strength. It signaled that you were blunt, real, unfiltered, and unbothered. Clean speech, on the other hand? That was for soft people, people who couldn't handle the heat, people who couldn't be trusted to keep up when things got raw.

That's how I saw it for years, and honestly, I bought into that lie pretty hard. I thought cussing made me sound tougher. Sharper. Like I had grit. Like I wasn't the guy you wanted to mess with. Maybe, in a way, it worked, maybe people did think twice before crossing me. But over time, I realized something unsettling. It wasn't just my enemies who were keeping their distance, it was the people I cared about, too.

See, words don't come with disclaimers. You can't speak harshly in one room and then expect people to assume you're gentle in another. If you lead with intensity everywhere you go, people stop expecting softness, even the ones who need it from you the most.

It's easy to be loud, it's easy to be sharp, but it takes real strength to be steady.

Now, I'm not saying we all need to talk like Sunday school teachers. This isn't about performing some artificial niceness but I am saying that the strongest people I've ever met — spiritually, emotionally, and mentally — aren't the ones who explode at every setback. They're the ones who know how to pause, how to hold a line without crossing it and how to speak with power *and* precision.

Jesus wasn't soft. He flipped tables. He called out hypocrites. He challenged corrupt systems, but He didn't lose control, he didn't cuss people out in the temple and he didn't walk around with a chip on His shoulder and a vocabulary to match. His strength was never in how loud He got, it was in how *intentional* He was.

That's the kind of strength I want. Not the kind that shouts to be heard, but the kind that's *respected because it's restrained*. Now, here's the part that surprised me, when I started toning down my language — not because someone made me, but because I wanted to — I didn't lose credibility. I gained it. People started to lean in. They noticed the shift, and even the ones who weren't believers started asking questions. "Why'd you stop talking like that?" "What changed?" "You okay?"

Those moments became opportunities, not just for conversation, but for connection.
Not once did someone say, "You know, I really miss the old angry version of you." Here's the bottom line. *You don't lose your edge when you clean up your mouth. You sharpen it.* You're not selling out. You're showing up — fully present, fully accountable, and fully aware of the power your words carry.

That's not weakness. That's wisdom.

"What If I Mess Up?" Grace for the Journey

> *But he said to me, "My grace is sufficient for you, for my power is perfected in weakness." Therefore, I will most gladly boast all the more about my weaknesses, so that Christ's power may reside in me.*
> *— 2 Corinthians 12:9*

Let's be real for a moment: you're going to mess up.

You're going to stub your toe. You're going to hit traffic when you're already late. You're going to drop your phone for the third time in a week, and something familiar is going to fly out of your mouth before your brain has time to catch it. When it does, that little voice in your head might whisper, "*Well, that's it. I blew it. I'm not cut out for this Christian stuff.*" Don't listen to that voice. It's lying. This journey you're on, of cleaning up your language, honoring God with your speech, rewiring decades of automatic responses, it's not about being perfect. It's about *progress*. It's about choosing growth over guilt, and grace over shame.

I've had moments, even years into following Jesus, where the old vocabulary came back like muscle memory. In a flash of stress or heat or anger, it would rise up before I had the chance to stop it, and in those moments, I didn't need a lecture. I didn't need someone quoting Leviticus at me. I needed a reminder that *this is a process*, and God is *still in it with me.* That's what Paul was talking about in 2 Corinthians. His weakness didn't disqualify him, it made space for grace. For power. For transformation. The same is true for you.

Slip-ups don't mean you're fake. They mean you're still being formed.

Sometimes, the mistake is actually the mirror. It shows you what's still in your heart, not to condemn you, but to *invite you* into deeper healing. You can't fix what you won't face, and you won't face it if you're afraid to be honest. This is why shame is so dangerous. It doesn't just make you feel bad, it isolates you. It convinces you that you're the only one struggling. That you're the only believer who still drops words you wish you hadn't and that's simply not true.

Every believer is in process. Some of us are working on pride. Others are working on patience. You might be working on your mouth and that's just as valid. The key is to stay *in the process*. To stay aware. To keep showing up, even after you stumble. Because the moment you decide, *"I want my words to match my walk,"* you've already begun the journey, and you don't have to walk it alone.

God isn't waiting for you to slip up so He can shake His head in disappointment. He's walking alongside you, gently helping you notice your patterns, rewrite your responses, and speak from a place of peace instead of panic. Grace isn't the backup plan, it's the *only* plan, and the more you lean into it, the more space you'll have to grow.

REFLECTION

What's Coming Out of You When You're Squeezed?

There's a saying in the culinary world: *What comes out of the pan is only as good as what you put into it.* You can't throw in bad ingredients and expect a beautiful dish. What's in the mix will always come through, especially under heat. The same goes for us. Pressure doesn't create character, it reveals it. Stress doesn't invent new words, it brings out the ones we've already rehearsed.

So when life turns up the heat, when the orders pile up, the table sends food back, the kid spills something right after you cleaned it, *what's coming out of you?* That's not a question to make you feel bad. It's a moment of invitation. Take a breath and ask yourself:

- When I'm frustrated, what words rise to the surface?

- Do I use language to defend myself, push others away, or blow off steam?

- Is my speech helping me grow, or just keeping me stuck in old patterns?

- What do I really believe about strength, and how does that show up in the way I speak?

You don't need to have perfect answers. This isn't a pop quiz, it's a pause. The more you notice what comes out of you when you're squeezed, the more clearly you'll see where God wants to bring healing. You're not too far gone, you're not behind, you're not the only one still wrestling. You're human, you're growing, and you're on the path.

With every small shift — every held tongue, every paused response, every ridiculous word swap that makes your kids laugh — you're creating new rhythms. New patterns. New pathways. You're building a language that reflects your new life. So keep going.

You don't need to be perfect to make a *Holy Shift*.

CHAPTER TWO: WHAT THE BIBLE ACTUALLY SAYS (AND WHAT IT DOESN'T)

"No foul language should come from your mouth, but only what is good for building up someone in need, so that it gives grace to those who hear."
— *Ephesians 4:29*

I had only been walking with Christ for a few months when it happened.

I'd just come out of the grocery store, arms full of bags, trying to maneuver through a packed parking lot with Oklahoma heat radiating off the blacktop like an open oven door. I was tired, hungry, and doing that awkward shuffle when your bags are cutting off circulation to your fingers and the only thing between you and air conditioning is fifty more steps and a broken cart return.

That's when a guy in a jacked-up pickup came barreling through the lot and cut right in front of me, nearly brushing my knees with his bumper. No horn. No hand signal. Just a quick rev and a "get out of my way" vibe. I flinched, nearly dropped my groceries, and instinctively let a sentence fly that would've made my old line cook buddies proud. Loud, clear, and colorful. Then, as if in slow motion, the driver looked up in his rearview mirror, and I looked down… at the back of my own car.

There it was, fresh from my new church, a big glossy sticker that said, **"Jesus Changed My Life."**

I wish I could tell you I immediately felt convicted. That I dropped to my knees in the parking lot and quoted Romans or sang a hymn. But honestly? My first thought was, *"Well, that's awkward."* My second thought was worse. *"I'm such a hypocrite."* I stood there, halfway between forgiveness and fury, watching this guy speed off while my words still echoed in my own ears. All I could think was, *"Man… what does the Bible actually say about this?"* That moment didn't ruin me, but it did *rattle* me. It was the first time I felt that strange tension between who I used to be and who I was trying to become. The language that had once felt like second nature suddenly felt out of place, like I was wearing old clothes that didn't quite fit anymore.

Now it wasn't because I got "caught." It was because I knew better now. Something in me *had* shifted, even if my vocabulary hadn't gotten the memo yet. That moment led me on a deeper search. Not for a list of "bad words," but for something more meaningful. I didn't just want cleaner language. I wanted *clarity*. I wanted to know what Scripture really says and doesn't say about the way we speak. I knew I wasn't alone. I knew there were others like me, trying to navigate this new life without faking it or white-knuckling their way into church-appropriate speech. People who loved Jesus but still had some kitchen and locker room left in them. People who had dropped old habits but still dropped a word or two when life hit hard.

So if that's you, welcome. This chapter's for us.

What the Bible Does (and Doesn't) Say

"Taming the Tongue… and Failing at It Daily"

> *"Death and life are in the power of the tongue, and those who love it will eat its fruit."* — *Proverbs 18:21*

When I first read this verse as a new believer, it hit me like a cast iron skillet to the conscience. (Which, by the way, I've actually experienced. Kitchens are war zones.) But this one didn't leave a bruise, it left a blueprint.

The Bible makes no secret about how powerful words are. They're not just sounds floating in the air. They're seeds. And seeds grow into something—blessing or destruction, encouragement or shame, hope or havoc. Proverbs is full of this kind of ancient, down-to-earth wisdom, and I've come to think of it as God's version of a kitchen manager's handbook. Short, blunt, sometimes a little sarcastic, but always spot-on.

The Tongue Has Power

Let's start with the heavy-hitters. Proverbs 18:21 tells us that *life and death* are in the power of the tongue. Not inconvenience and awkwardness. Life and death. That's a big claim for something that weighs about 2.5 ounces.

James 3 doubles down and basically says the tongue is a wild animal that no one can tame, like a rogue raccoon in your prayer closet. It's full of deadly poison. It sets whole forests on fire. And it's somehow still in your mouth while you're singing praises to God and then snapping at a barista for getting your oat milk order wrong. (Been there. Twice. Same barista.)

The Bible doesn't let us off the hook. But it doesn't beat us over the head either. What it offers is clarity and a challenge to take responsibility.

Build Up, Don't Tear Down

Paul says in **Ephesians 4:29**:

> *"No foul language should come from your mouth, but only what is good for building up someone in need, so that it gives grace to those who hear."*

And in **Colossians 4:6**:

> *"Let your speech always be gracious, seasoned with salt, so that you may know how you should answer each person."*

(Seasoned with salt? Now that's my kind of verse. Shoutout to the culinary ministry.)

Paul's not handing out a list of banned vocabulary. He's pointing to purpose. Is your language helpful? Is it gracious? Is it making things better, or just louder? These are the questions that matter.

Jesus Gets to the Heart

Jesus, as usual, goes straight past the behavior and pokes at the heart. In **Luke 6:45**, He says:

> *"A good person produces good out of the good stored up in his heart. An evil person produces evil out of the evil stored up in his heart, for his mouth speaks from the overflow of the heart."*

In other words, your mouth isn't just a muscle, it's a mirror. Whatever's sloshing around in your heart is going to splash out of your lips. Which explains a lot about the things I've said after stubbing my toe or spilling a fryer basket of chicken tenders on my crocs.

This isn't about legalism. This is about overflow. If you're full of anger, frustration, bitterness—or just plain stress, it's going to show up in your language. Not because you're evil, but because you're leaking.

What the Bible Doesn't Say

Now, let's be real for a minute. The Bible doesn't give us a printed-out list of curse words to avoid. You can't find a verse that says, "Thou shalt not drop an F-bomb when thou spillest thy coffee."

You know what else it doesn't say? It doesn't say that God is waiting to zap you every time you say a word that rhymes with "duck." He's not a grammar cop. He's a heart surgeon. His concern is where your words are coming from and what they're doing to the people around you.

It's not about syllables. It's about **impact** and **intent**. Did your words crush or comfort? Did they glorify God or glorify your anger? Did they shift the atmosphere or just add static?

God's not nitpicking your vocabulary. He's inviting you to **speak with purpose**. To become aware of the *why* behind the *what*. Honestly, anybody can clean up their mouth for a job interview, but can you do it when life punches you in the patience?

This is the shift we're after. Not just cleaner speech, but

deeper awareness. Language that doesn't just avoid "bad words," but chooses better ones. On purpose. With heart. In alignment with the One who gave us the gift of language in the first place.

So let's bust a few myths:

- **Myth #1: "There are holy words and unholy words."**
  Not exactly. There are *holy intentions* and *unholy impacts*, but language evolves. What was scandalous in one era becomes casual in another. The point is never the specific word, it's what it does to the person hearing it and what it reveals in the speaker's heart.

- **Myth #2: "God is counting your slip-ups."**
  God's not sitting in heaven with a red pen grading your speech like a substitute teacher. He's after your heart, and He knows sanctification is a *process*. You're not expected to go from sailor to saint overnight.

- **Myth #3: "If I use a substitute word, I'm still sinning."**
  Not if your substitute avoids harm, honors others, and helps you self-regulate. In fact, that kind of intentional self-control is part of spiritual maturity. More on this in future chapters.

Cussing, Cursing, and Coarse Joking: What's the Difference?

We throw around words like "cussing" and "cursing" like they're the same thing — but biblically speaking, they're as different as a stubbed toe and a vindictive voodoo chant. And then there's coarse joking, which might sneak in under the radar but still hits just as hard in the heart. Let's break it down without sounding like a church sign from 1994.

Cussing: The Reflexive Release

This is the one most of us are tangled up in. You smash your finger with a hammer, boom. You're not speaking in tongues. You're speaking in *four-letter interpretations of pain.* **Cussing** is what we typically think of as modern profanity. It's crude. It's emotional. It's often tied to stress, pain, frustration, or that one guy who *still* won't use his blinker. It's not usually premeditated. It's the knee-jerk of language, like your words are trying to punch the problem in the face, but here's the key: **it's not always meant to harm**, it's often just meant to *vent*. While it might feel harmless, what comes out of us under pressure says a lot about what's inside us.

Cursing: The Verbal Hit Job

Cursing, in the biblical sense, is way more serious. This isn't you yelling at a red light. This is you *calling down harm on someone*. Think of it like speaking a spiritual sucker punch. You're wishing pain, ruin, or failure on somebody, even if you're not chanting in Latin with candles. Old-school biblical cursing was invoking real damage, destruction, condemnation, judgment. While we may not word it that way today, some of our "venting" still leans dangerously close to it. Ever said something like? "I hope they get what's coming to them." "Karma'll catch 'em." "God's gonna strike them down." Sounds righteous, but it's not. Jesus calls us to **bless our enemies**, not roast them in holy oil.

Coarse Joking: The Laugh That Leaves a Bruise

Ah, yes. **Coarse joking**. This one's sneaky, because it hides behind humor, but just because people laugh doesn't mean it wasn't a hit. Paul specifically calls this out in Ephesians 5:4:

> *"Obscene and foolish talking or crude joking are not suitable, but rather giving thanks."*

Coarse joking includes sexual innuendo, humor that disrespects others, and the kind of sarcasm that stops being clever and starts being cruel. It's the kind of joke that gets laughs at someone else's expense. It's "just kidding," but not really. Humor should lift the room, not lower the bar. If the Spirit in you cringes while the room cackles, that's worth listening to.

So, What's the Big Deal?

It's not just about **which** words we use, it's about **what spirit is driving them**.

- Cussing often flows from stress, but reveals our **reflex**.

- Cursing flows from judgment, and reveals our **heart**.

- Coarse joking flows from pride or pain, and reveals what we **think is okay** to laugh at.

God's concern isn't about whether your sentence includes a spicy syllable, it's whether your words are **life-giving or toxic. Are they building someone up or breaking them down?** Are they rooted in love, or marinated in sarcasm and self-justification? This doesn't mean you need to sound like a Christian Hallmark card 24/7. It means we take responsibility for the wake our words leave behind. Because there's always a wake.

God's Not Mad at Your Mouth, He's After Your Heart

He's not nitpicking every slip-up. He's looking deeper, at what's driving your words in the first place.

> *"Humans do not see what the Lord sees, for humans see what is visible, but the Lord sees the heart." -1 Samuel 16:7*

Let's take a deep breath here. This whole conversation? It's not about becoming some kind of Christian language robot. It's not about God standing over you with a divine swear jar, waiting to ding you a nickel every time you slip. (If that were the case, I'd be spiritually bankrupt and emotionally overdrafted.) God's not mad at your mouth. He's after your heart. That's the whole deal. He's not focused on the syllables you spit out when you stub your toe or miss a turn. He's focused on what's spilling out from the inside. Our language is just a loud, messy echo of what's happening deeper down — our stress, our sarcasm, our pride, our pain, our honesty, and sometimes our humanity just... leaking. Luke 6:45 isn't about lip service. It's about heart condition. It's Jesus saying: *If you want to clean up what's coming out, you've got to pay attention to what's going in.* When it comes to cleaning up our language? That's where the shift really starts.

Growth Isn't Polished, It's Awkward (And Sometimes Hilarious)

Let me tell you about the time I tried to "talk holy" in front of a table full of youth pastors. It was early in my faith walk. I'd been saved a few months, maybe less. I was still working in the kitchen, still had burns on my arms and attitude in my blood, but I was trying hard, like, *really* hard, to sound "transformed." So I'm at this dinner, sitting with this crew of church staff, and one guy spills his drink on the table. Without thinking, I blurt out.

"Ah, bless his heart, may the Lord soak up that iced tea like the blood of the Lamb!"...What? Even I didn't know what I meant. I was trying to replace my usual go-to phrases with something spiritual, but what came out sounded like a mix of Southern grandma, televangelist, and confused waiter.

The room was quiet. Then someone chuckled. Then another, and suddenly we were all laughing, not at *me*, but with me. Because every single one of them had a story just like it. Moments when they tried to "talk clean," "sound churchy," or "say the right thing," and it just didn't quite land. Here's the thing. That moment wasn't wasted, it was part of the process. It was awkward, sure, but it was also *authentic.* It showed that my heart was aiming in a new direction, even if my mouth hadn't caught up yet.

Real Talk: God's After Alignment, Not Perfection

This shift we're making, from cursing to blessing, from sarcasm to truth, from reflex to reflection, it's not about perfection. It's about *alignment.* You don't have to memorize a list of substitute words and deploy them like a well-trained vocabulary ninja. You don't have to filter every syllable through a WWJD translator. You're not being asked to perform. You're being invited to *transform.* God's desire isn't to police your phrases, it's to heal the places they come from. He knows we're works in progress. He knows you're going to drop a jar of marinara on the kitchen floor and something spicy is going to come out of your mouth. He's not in heaven muttering, "Wow. Strike one, Buz." He's not disappointed. He's *developing you,* and trust me, He's got patience. A lot more than you have for that one guy who always cuts you off in traffic.

Where We're Headed

So if you've messed up, you're in the right place. If you've tried to sound better and just ended up sounding weird? Still the right place. If you've felt discouraged because your words haven't caught up with your heart yet? Welcome to the club and take heart. This isn't about changing who you are. It's about becoming more of who God made you to be — on purpose, with words that reflect the shift that's happening inside. Your mouth might still drop the occasional expletive, but your heart? That's where the holy work is happening. And holy shift, it's already starting.

What Clean Speech Isn't

Let's get something straight. Clean speech does not mean becoming a Christian Mr. Rogers. You're not expected to wear a cardigan, talk in hushed tones, and say "golly gee" every time you drop a can of beans on your foot. In fact, one of the quickest ways to make people tune out, especially people who don't know Jesus yet, is to come off like a walking, talking episode of a 1950s sitcom. It's not real and people can smell fake a mile away.

Clean speech isn't about being "nice" 24/7. It's not about pretending you're not frustrated when you are. It's not about suppressing your anger or grief or pain like it doesn't exist. It's about ownership. It's about choosing to be intentional, not reactive, with the words you say. It's about being real without being reckless. It's about letting your mouth reflect your maturity, not just your mood. You can be righteously angry and still stay aligned with who you're becoming. You can express deep sorrow, frustration, even sharp truth and do it in a way that honors God *and* respects people. Scripture doesn't say, "Don't feel things." It says, "Be angry, but do not sin" (Eph. 4:26). That means your emotions are valid, but your actions (and words) still matter.

Think of it like this. Clean speech isn't a muzzle, it's a microphone. It amplifies who you are or who you're becoming. Not perfectly, but purposefully. It's not about scrubbing out your personality or turning down your volume. It's about tuning your voice to a better station. One that builds, blesses, and brings life.

REFLECTION

How Do You Use Your Words?

Before you close this chapter and go back into the chaos of dropped pans, missed turns, or messy Mondays, pause for a second. Let's get real. How are your words shaping the world around you? Are they building? Breaking? Are they aligned with who you're becoming or just spilling out unchecked from old habits?

Take a moment to reflect:

- **Do my words reflect who I'm becoming or just who I've been?**

- **Am I building others up, or just reacting to whatever's in front of me?**

- **What kind of influence do I want to have when I speak even in heated moments?**

This isn't about sounding "Christian." It's about sounding like someone who's been changed. Someone who's learning, stumbling, growing, and still full of life. Someone who can drop a spoon and still bless the room. There's no shame in the journey, just an open invitation. Let your words reflect the shift happening in your heart. It won't be perfect, but it will be powerful.

CHAPTER THREE: THE DANGIT DILEMMA: WHY CLEAN WORDS FEEL SO WEIRD (AT FIRST)

"Let your speech always be gracious, seasoned with salt, so that you may know how you should answer each person." — Colossians 4:6

There's nothing quite like the moment you drop something heavy, stub your toe, or find yourself staring at a $400 mechanic bill and all you can manage to mutter is: "Aw, fudge."It just doesn't hit the same. At first, trying to clean up your language feels like swapping out your favorite boots for a pair of stiff church shoes. It's awkward. It's uncomfortable. And it feels like everyone can tell you're faking it. Here's the thing, that's normal. Seriously. You're not broken. You're just in the "word detox" stage. It's a little weird, a little clunky, and it takes some trial and error to find phrases that feel like you.

I remember when I first started trying to change how I talked, especially when I was working in kitchens. Kitchens aren't exactly monasteries, if you know what I mean. I'd been a chef, an athlete, and a bounty hunter. Three environments where swearing is practically a second language. It was like breathing. You didn't even think about it, it just flew out.

So imagine the first time I dropped a full pan of chicken stock and tried to substitute "dagnabbit." Yeah. That didn't land. Not with the crew. Not with me. I felt like Yosemite Sam trying to lead a prayer meeting. The shift felt forced at first. Like I was trying to play a character and for a minute, I almost gave up. Here's what helped, I stopped trying to sound like somebody else and started finding words and reactions that still felt *real*, just more *intentional*. So instead of blurting out the classics, I started reaching for phrases like:
"C'mon!"

"You gotta be kidding me."
"Are you serious right now?"
"What in the world?"

They weren't fake. They were still *me*, just not fueled by rage or flying expletives. They bought me a second to breathe. They reminded me that I wasn't a slave to my first reaction and they gave me space to choose. Over time, that choice became more automatic.

Why It Feels So Weird at First

Let's talk brain science for a second. Swear words live in the emotional part of your brain, the limbic system. That's why they feel so good when you're mad or in pain. They're fast, primal, and explosive. Replacement words, though? They come from the prefrontal cortex, the part of your brain that plans, filters, and regulates. That means clean speech has to be *intentional* at first. You're rewiring your responses. That takes time. It's like switching from muscle memory to manual control. You're not just changing your *words*, you're changing your *automatic settings*.

And that's no small thing.

So if "dangit" feels flat and "golly" makes you cringe, you're not alone. You're just in the early stages of "linguistic rehab." It's like learning to walk again after years of sprinting with bad form. It's clumsy. It's awkward. Sometimes you mumble out a "shoot-a-doodle" and immediately question your life choices.

Let's be honest: not every substitute fits. Some of them feel like you're borrowing your grandma's vocabulary, and some make you sound like a Disney character trying to cuss someone out in a G-rated movie. But here's the good news, you don't have to settle for "dangit" if it doesn't fit you. This isn't about becoming Ned Flanders with a thesaurus. It's about staying *you*, just a more thoughtful, present, grounded version of you.

Finding Words That Actually Sound Like You

Start with how you already talk. If you're the type to say "You've got to be kidding me" when something goes sideways, lean into that. That counts! You're already using your own natural substitution, it's not fake, not forced, just *filtered*.

Here are a few more real-life examples:

- **"What in the world?"** — Classic. Southern. Works for just about any surprise from a broken faucet to a toddler with peanut butter in their eyebrows.

- **"Seriously?"** — Drips with passive-aggressive energy. Effective in traffic or when someone cuts in line at Chick-fil-A.

- **"C'mon, man…"** — Sports background gold. Just enough edge without being toxic.

- **"Okay. Cool. That's how we're living now."** — Great for broken printers, spilled smoothies, or when someone rear-ends you and blames *you*.

When you can't find the right words? **Make them up.** (Trust me, I do it all the time.) Ever shout *"Sweet mother of meatballs!"* after burning your hand on a hot pan? Or mutter *"Fluffernutter"* when you dropped your phone face-down? These kinds of words are goofy, yes, lol, but they interrupt your brain's old loop. They stop the autopilot. That moment of disruption? That's your in, that's where you get to choose a better response.

The Psychology of Why Substitutions Work

When you say something different, even if it's silly or weird, you're teaching your brain a new habit loop. And you're lowering the emotional temperature in the room (or in your head). Swear words escalate. Substitutes *interrupt*.

Psychologists call this a **pattern interrupt**, a way to derail a conditioned response and replace it with a new one. So when your go-to F-bomb gets replaced with a dramatic *"For the love of gravy!"* or *"Mercy me!"*, it's not just a goofy phrase. It's a rewiring cue. It's your brain learning that there's more than one way to respond, and that learning matters.

The more you interrupt the old habit, the weaker it gets. The more you use a new one, the stronger it becomes. Eventually, you won't have to think so hard about it. It'll feel more natural. More *you*.

The 'Fake Christian' Fear

A lot of folks back off the clean-speech journey because they feel phony when they try and I get that. When you've spent your whole life expressing yourself a certain way — raw, unfiltered, and loud — it can feel disingenuous to suddenly swap "$#@!" for "gosh darn."

I've had people tell me, "I don't want to sound like I'm pretending. That's not me." Here's the thing, **just because something doesn't feel natural *yet* doesn't mean it's not *authentic*.**

Growth always feels foreign at first. When I started

working out again after years away from the gym, everything felt stiff and awkward. My form was off. I looked ridiculous. But over time, it became natural — not because I was faking, but because I kept showing up. Your vocabulary is the same way. It takes practice. Rewiring. Intention. And sometimes... a little awkwardness.

Identity vs. Expression

Here's what's really at stake: **the tension between who you've been and who you're becoming.** When you start filtering your words, it feels like you're leaving part of yourself behind, but maybe that's not a bad thing. Maybe you're just letting go of what no longer fits.

I had a friend who used to say, "I'll stop cussing when Jesus returns." Funny guy. But behind that joke was something deeper, he thought cleaning up his mouth would make him boring, soft, or fake. That it would mean giving up his edge. What he didn't realize was this. His *edge* wasn't his profanity. It was his **passion**, and passion doesn't disappear when you stop cussing, it just finds a better mic. You don't lose who you are when you clean up your speech. You uncover who you're becoming.

The Real Reason You're Shifting

This whole journey isn't about impressing your pastor, your small group, or the homeschool mom next door. It's about **alignment**. Getting your words to match the shift happening inside you. The more you grow, the less you'll want to sound like your old self, not because someone told you to clean it up, but because it no longer fits who you are. Like trying to wear your high school football jersey at 40. You could... but why?

As Proverbs reminds us again and again, our words have the power to build, destroy, protect, ignite, calm, provoke, or heal. They reflect the condition of our heart and they help shape the hearts around us. So maybe "dangit" still sounds a little dorky to you. That's fine. You're not married to it. You're just in training. Try something else. Test out a few that feel fun, real, *you*. (We'll give you a whole A-to-Z list later in this book.)

But don't give up just because it feels weird. Weird is the hallway between old habits and new freedom.

REFLECTION

What Sounds Like You?

Let's get real. Nobody cleans up their language by accident. This takes intention and a little creativity, but it doesn't have to feel fake or forced. You're not trying to win a "Most Wholesome" award... you're just trying to stop sounding like you crashed your cart into the gates of hell every time you drop a frozen pizza on the floor. So take a second and think through this:

1. What Are *Your* Trigger Moments?

- When do the words fly out without a filter?

    - Dropping something?

    - Getting cut off in traffic?

    - Technology glitching like it has a personal vendetta?

    - Kids breaking something... again?

Write those moments down. You can't change what you don't notice.

2. What Feels Natural Coming Out of Your Mouth?

Say a few of these out loud:

- "C'mon, man."
- "Are you kidding me?"
- "What in the WORLD was that?"
- "Sheesh."
- "Dang, that stings."
- "You've got to be kidding me."
- "Well, bless it all."
- "Nope. Not today."

Which ones made you laugh? Which ones felt awkward? Which ones actually helped you let off steam? Start collecting the ones that *work*. Make your own list. Keep it handy. Try using one a day until it starts to feel like second nature.

3. What's One Phrase You Can Retire This Week?

Pick one of your go-to expletives and say goodbye (for now). Replace it with one of your new "you-sounding" options. Catch yourself. Laugh when you slip. And remember: this isn't about perfection, it's about practice.

CHAPTER FOUR: HOW TO CATCH IT BEFORE YOU SHOUT IT

"A fool gives full vent to his anger, but a wise person holds it in check." — Proverbs 29:11

Let's be honest, some days feel like a trap designed to see how fast you can go from "blessed and highly favored" to "one wrong move from a meltdown." You wake up with the best intentions, maybe even whisper a prayer as your feet hit the floor...and then you step on a Lego, or a glittery unicorn hair clip, or your kid's fake makeup kit that's now fused to the tile with grape juice. Maybe you spill coffee down the front of your clean shirt on the exact morning you're already running late. Or you hit every single red light between your house and wherever you *really didn't want to go in the first place.* In that flash of frustration, in that one micro-moment between trigger and reaction, out it comes. The automatic response, the knee-jerk phrase, the expletive that's been lurking just beneath the surface. Not because you're a bad person, but because *that's the groove your brain has carved over the years.* It's familiar, fast, and (let's face it) oddly satisfying in the moment.

But this chapter isn't about feeling guilty for those moments. It's about *getting in front of them.*

Language Is a Habit and Habits Can Be Hacked

Most of us don't think about our language until after the words have already escaped our lips. That's because habitual speech is tied to our **limbic system**, the emotional part of the brain. When something triggers you (pain, anger, surprise), the limbic system doesn't send the situation to your logic center for approval. It defaults to what you've always done. That go-to word or phrase that's been used so often, it practically has a parking spot in your mouth.

This is why shouting "What the heck?!" when someone cuts you off in traffic feels almost involuntary. It *is*, at first. But here's the good news, habits are built... and they can be rebuilt.

What neuroscience tells us and what Scripture reinforces is that we are capable of transformation. Romans 12:2 doesn't say "Try harder not to curse." It says, "Be transformed by the renewing of your mind." Transformation means a new default setting, not just white-knuckling your way through frustration.

Know Your Triggers

One of the biggest keys to changing habitual language is recognizing the moments that set you off. For some of us, it's physical pain. Stub a toe, smash a thumb, and the tongue unleashes its fury. For others, it's stress, traffic, or feeling disrespected. Maybe it's being late, overwhelmed, hungry, or — let's just admit it — all of the above at once. Take inventory of what makes you feel like you're about to erupt. You're not trying to avoid life's annoyances (good luck with that); you're trying to *become aware of them before they take the wheel.*

The more familiar you are with your personal pressure points, the more equipped you'll be to insert a pause before reacting. That pause doesn't just save your mouth, it saves your witness.

Create Pause Points and Pattern Interrupts

Jesus wasn't surprised by people's reactions. He knew what was in their hearts and He often responded not with fire, but with *a question*, or *a pause*. That's powerful.

When your default response wants to rush to the surface, experiment with "pause points." These are intentional moments where you stop, breathe, and make space for a different reaction. Even a two-second pause can be enough to derail a verbal trainwreck. A "pattern interrupt" is a tool used in psychology to break a cycle, and it works with speech, too. Some people snap a rubber band on their wrist (don't worry, we're not suggesting self-inflicted pain). Others use a keyword or phrase like, "C'mon now," or "Seriously?" or even a silent prayer: *Lord, take this from my mouth before I launch it like a grenade.*

Try this: Next time you feel yourself heading toward a verbal spiral, say "Not today." Even that small act can interrupt your pattern just long enough to choose a different word or no word at all.

Prayer in the Moment

It doesn't have to be a long, eloquent monologue. Just a simple, honest breath prayer can redirect your mind and body. "Help me, Lord." "Give me grace." "Hold my tongue and my attitude."

God isn't asking you to be a robot. He's inviting you to partner with Him in reshaping your inner world because the words will follow. Luke 6:45 puts it clearly, "A good person produces good out of the good stored up in his heart. An evil person produces evil out of the evil stored up in his heart, for his mouth speaks from the overflow of the heart." Translation? You don't need to duct tape your lips. You need to flood your heart with better stuff and your mouth will eventually catch up.

Real Growth Happens in Real Life

Don't wait until you feel perfectly calm or super spiritual to practice. The goal isn't to create a serene monastery inside your SUV, it's to train your brain and heart in the middle of the real, messy, frustrating stuff. You'll still mess up sometimes. We all do, but you'll also start to catch those moments a little earlier. You'll find that the pause gets longer. The new phrase comes quicker. And the feeling of regret gets replaced by a sense of progress, even if you're just inching forward.

This isn't about having a perfectly clean mouth. It's about building a new reflex and one that reflects who you're becoming, not just where you've been.

REFLECTION

What's Coming Out of Your Mouth and Why?

This isn't about perfection. It's about paying attention. You don't need to become a speech-monitoring robot. You just need to grow in awareness — and invite God into the process. As you think about the last few days or even the last few hours, reflect on this:

- When I react emotionally, what kind of language tends to come out?

- Are there specific triggers that send me into verbal autopilot?

- What does my word choice reveal about what's going on in my heart?

- Have I practiced pause points — or am I just pressing play and letting it rip?

- How might prayer or a breath in the moment shift my default response?

Try not to overanalyze. Just notice. Be curious, not critical, and remember, the goal here isn't just cleaner language. It's a clearer reflection of who you're becoming. You're not trying to impress anyone. You're aligning your heart with something (and Someone) greater. So the next time the coffee spills, the tire blows, or your kid dumps their entire Happy Meal into the backseat, don't aim for perfection. Aim for pause. Progress. Presence.

Even a quiet "Help me, Jesus" counts as a win.

CHAPTER FIVE: ALPHABETICAL OUTBURSTS (THAT WON'T GET YOU KICKED OUT OF BIBLE STUDY)

"The one who guards his mouth protects his life; the one who opens his lips invites his own ruin." — Proverbs 13:3

A–Z of Sanctified Substitutes

A survival guide for your mouth.

You ever stub your toe on the coffee table and shout "crud muffins" at 6:30 a.m. while trying not to wake the whole house? Welcome. You're one of us now. Let's be honest, the hardest part of cleaning up your language isn't knowing *why* to do it. It's figuring out *what in the world* to say instead. For those of us who grew up in locker rooms, kitchens, construction crews, or just high-stress households… tame alternatives can feel downright ridiculous. You know the feeling. You try to say "golly" and immediately want to punch yourself in the throat.

That's why this chapter exists. It's not about being cute or Sunday-schooly. It's about giving you options, lots of them. Funny ones. Realistic ones. Faith-tinged-but-not-cringe ones. And some that are so weird they actually work. Use them. Modify them. Make them your own.

Ready? Let's go from A to Z. Because your mouth deserves a

toolkit.

A

- **Ah, biscuits!** (Southern sass meets pastry panic.)
- **Applesauce!** (Wholesome and confusing.)
- **Aw, c'mon!** (Universal disappointment, clean edition.)

B

- **Bless it all!** (Righteous. Frustrated. Effective.)
- **Bologna sandwich!** (Pairs well with "What the—")
- **Buckets!** (Short. Sharp. Still satisfying.)

C

- **Crud muffins!** (Don't knock it till you try it.)
- **Cheddar and Pickles!** (It's the chef in me.)
- **Come on, man!** (Disbelief with a Michael Scott vibe.)

D

- **Don't do it today!** (When you're feeling on edge..)
- **Dagnabbit!** (Old-school but still kicking.)

- **Donut hole!** (Versatile and weirdly fun to yell.)

E

- **Excuse my everything.** (When you're being clumsy.)
- **Everything but the kitchen sink!** (When chaos reigns.)
- **Excuse me, what now?** (Perfect for absurd moments.)

F

- **Fudge buckets!** (Sweet. Still expressive.)
- **Fiddlesticks!** (Old-school, but has comedic charm.)
- **For crying out loud!** (Reliable classic.)

G

- **Good gravy!** (Pairs well with holiday stress.)
- **Gosh darnit!** (Squeaky-clean but still firm.)
- **Great googly moogly!** (The louder, the better.)

H

- **Heck fire!** (Midwest favorite.)
- **Holy smokes!** (Good for surprises.)
- **Here we go!** (For nonsense and general irritation.)

I

- **I kid you not.** (Strong disbelief.)
- **I swear on a stack of pancakes.** (A creative oath.)
- **I'm tellin' you what...** (Southern moms everywhere.)

J

- **Jiminy Christmas!** (Mild and old-school.)
- **Jumpin' Jehoshaphat!** (Theatrical, but it plays.)
- **Jellybeans!** (Ridiculous. Embrace it.)

K

- **Kiss my grits!** (Thanks, Flo from *Alice*.)
- **Krakatoa!** (Explosive, literally.)
- **Kidding me right now?!** (Modern & useful.)

L

- **Landsakes!** (Vintage charm.)
- **Lemon squeeze!** (Oddly satisfying.)
- **Lord, help me.** (Also counts as a prayer.)

M

- **Mercy!** (For when it's just *too much*.)
- **Mother of pearl!** (Timeless and dramatic.)
- **My word!** (Short and sharp.)

N

- **No sir!** / **No ma'am!** (Good all-purpose refusal.)
- **Nuts!** (Simple, quick, and still packs a punch.)
- **No way, José!** (Rhyming always softens the blow.)

O

- **Oh, snap!** (Still cool. Still works.)
- **Oh, bless it!** (Soft and prayer-adjacent.)

- **Oh, for Pete's sake!** (We still don't know who Pete is.)

P

- **Pickle juice!** (Unexpected and spicy.)
- **Phooey!** (Cartoonish but classic.)
- **Pardon my tone.** (Great reset phrase.)

Q

- **Quack attack!** (Chaos in bird form.)
- **Quiet down, ya hooligans!** (Parental gold.)
- **Questionable choices!** (When life goes sideways.)

R

- **Rats!** (Minimalist regret.)
- **Razzle frazzle!** (Old-timey irritation.)
- **Really?!** (Pain, meet humor.)

S

- **Shiitake mushrooms!** (You already knew.)
- **Son of a biscuit!** (Classic bait-and-switch.)

- **Snapdragon!** (Sounds floral. Feels fierce.)

T

- **Tarnation!** (Frontier frustration.)
- **Thunderation!** (Rare but powerful.)
- **Tell me I didn't...** (Self-roast approved.)

U

- **Unbelievable!** (Tried-and-true.)
- **Ugh, seriously?!** (Great in traffic.)
- **Up a creek!** (Don't finish the sentence.)

V

- **Vanilla fudge!** (Mild but tasty.)
- **Varmints!** (Old-school insult for small annoyances.)
- **Victory is not looking good.** (Accepting your fate.)

W

- **What in the world?!** (Your go-to.)
- **Well, butter my biscuits.** (Confusion meets charm.)
- **Who does that?!** (Every day, probably.)

X

- **Xeorox cop!** (Nonsense. That's the point.)
- **Xtra grace needed.** (When you're barely holding it together.)
- **X marks the moment I lost my cool.** (Narrate your spiral.)

Y

- **Yikes!** (Short and effective.)
- **You gotta be kidding me!** (Use daily.)
- **You better hush.** (Southern heat incoming.)

Z

- **Zippity doo-dah!** (Ironically furious.)
- **Zucchini!** (Anger made snackable.)
- **Zero chill. That's me.** (Own it.)

There is always the old school ones to use, for example: Dang it, heck and shoot. These are just some alternatives to help change it up.

How to Make Your Own Holy Shift Phrases

Now that you've seen what's possible when biscuits and mushrooms become your go-to instead of bombs and blasphemy, it's time to give you the keys to the kingdom, how to come up with your *own* clean-but-satisfying expressions that sound like *you*. Not some Stepford Christian. Not Ned Flanders. *You*.

Because let's face it: saying "fudge buckets" is hilarious, until you've said it 800 times in a week. It starts to lose its punch. That's why you need a rotating cast of phrases that match your personality, region, and sense of humor.

1. Start With Your Tone

Are you sarcastic? Sweet? Dry? Dramatic? Great. Lean into it.

- If you're sarcastic, try stuff like:
  "Oh, brilliant move, genius."
  "Well, that's just spectacular."
  "I must be cursed by the sock-folding gods."

- If you're sweet-natured but stressed:
  "Heavens to Betsy, not again."
  "Good gravy."
  "Oh, bless my buttons."

- If you're more no-nonsense:
  "Cut it out."
  "C'mon now."
  "Don't do it today."

2. Borrow From Where You're From

Southern folks have an endless supply of clean (but spicy)

phrases:
"She's madder than a wet hen."
"Well butter my biscuits."
"Bless your heart… sideways."

Northerners? Try the blunt-and-understated route:
"Oh, for crying out loud."
"You've got to be kidding me."
"This is ridiculous."

West Coasters? Channel your inner laid-back surfer or high-strung tech bro:
"Bro… seriously?"
"What in the actual Wi-Fi outage is this?"
"Namaste… not today."

3. Make It Physical

One of the most underrated tricks? Pair your words with a funny *gesture* or facial expression. Roll your eyes. Clutch your heart dramatically. Mime throwing something. Sometimes the *way* you say it makes all the difference.

4. Give Yourself Permission to Sound Weird at First

You're going to feel awkward the first few times. That's normal. New words are like new shoes, they might give you blisters at first. Doesn't mean they're not a better fit in the long run. The point isn't perfection. It's progress. It's rewiring your reflexes so that when life hits you with a sledgehammer moment, your mouth doesn't add shrapnel.

REFLECTION

Finding Your Voice Without Losing Your Mind

You made it through a full buffet of biscuits, fudge buckets, and shiitake mushrooms and somehow, you're still here. Still you. Still just as expressive, just maybe a little less... explosive. Let's take a moment and sit with what we've learned, not just about the *words*, but about *you*. Language is personal. It's wrapped in memory, culture, emotion, and rhythm. So when we shift the way we speak, even just a little, it can feel weird. Like moving furniture in the dark. You bump into stuff. You question why you even started. But if you've ever dropped something in the kitchen and heard yourself shout a new phrase that didn't include a federal offense... that's progress. If you've paused for one extra second and *chosen* your words instead of defaulting to old patterns... that's victory. If you've laughed at yourself mid-sentence because you yelled, "Son of a brisket!" in traffic... that's growth.

So let's reflect:

◆ **What phrases from this chapter made you laugh out loud?**
Write them down. Stick them on your fridge. Make them

yours.

◆ **Which ones felt natural to you and which felt like trying on someone else's shoes?**
It's okay to ditch the ones that don't fit. The goal isn't to sound like me. It's to sound like *you*… cleaned up, but still fully you.

◆ **Think back to the last time you dropped something, stubbed a toe, or missed a turn.**
What did you say? What *could* you have said?

◆ **Can you come up with 3 original phrases that are totally your style?**
Try blending your favorite foods, weird family sayings, or inside jokes. You're not just editing your mouth, you're designing your own soundboard.

Swapping out your go-to words isn't about becoming someone else. It's about reclaiming your voice. One holy shift at a time.

CHAPTER SIX: WHAT TO SAY WHEN YOU DROP A PAN, MISS A TURN, OR SLAM A FINGER

"A gentle answer turns away anger, but a harsh word stirs up wrath." — Proverbs 15:1

There's a moment, right after the impact but before the words fly ,where time slows down. The pan hits the floor. The toe finds the coffee table. The GPS reroutes... again... for the third time this morning.In that microsecond, your mouth is like a fighter jet on standby. The words? Oh, they're ready. Locked. Loaded. Unholy. This chapter is for *that moment*. The real-life, real-stress, real-loud moments when your first instinct is to launch a full verbal airstrike and you're trying *so hard* not to. Because let's be real, the challenge isn't just *not cussing in theory.* It's not cussing when your lasagna hits the oven door and explodes into a cheesy volcano of doom.

When You Burn Yourself (Or Anything Else)

Burns aren't just physical. They're emotional. Especially if it's your third one this week and all you wanted was a grilled cheese. **You might normally say,** a four-letter phrase involving mothers, unholy fire, or Satan's sauna.

Try this instead:

- "Holy jalapeños!"

- "Ow, biscuits on a barbecue!"

- "I rebuke this oven in the name of Jesus!"

"Be angry and do not sin; do not let the sun go down on your anger." — Ephesians 4:26

Because you can be mad... and still make it holy (or at least mildly entertaining).

When You Miss a Turn, Hit Traffic, or Get Cut Off

Driving is basically a spiritual boot camp. Your patience,

kindness, and vocabulary are all tested in real-time. Blessings to every backseat driver and blinker-denier. **You might normally say,**
A mix of pirate, sailor, and demon-summoning incantations.

Try this instead:

- "Well butter my biscuit and call me lost."

- "Turnip trucks! I missed it again."

- "Well here we go again."

Instead of escalating, breathe. Shift your tone. Add humor. You're not stuck, you're rerouted for a reason.

When You Drop Something Loud and Fragile

Nothing awakens the mouth demons like a shattered plate or a splattered smoothie. **You might normally say,** let's be honest, you black out and regain consciousness mid-cleanup.

Try this instead:

- "Mother of pearl onions!"

- "Praise break! That was close."

- "Well... that plate's with Jesus now."

If you've got kids or coworkers nearby, you just bought yourself five stars on the family-friendly vocabulary chart.

When You Stub, Slam, Slice, or Step on Something

This is the kind of pain that shoots straight to your soul. Toe vs. bedpost. Thumb vs. hammer. Lego vs. bare foot. **You might normally say,** a combination of yelling and inventing new curse dialects.

Try this instead:

- "Not today, Satan's furniture!"

- "Crickets on a pogo stick!"

- "Lord, lay hands on my foot right now."

It's not weird to pray through pain. Even if it's just, "Jesus, help me not lose it." That counts.

When Someone Else Pushes Your Buttons

You didn't drop a pan, you dropped your *cool*. And that counts, too. **You might normally say:**
Nothing at first. Just a long, simmering silence... then an outburst.

Try this instead:

- "Help me, Holy Spirit."

- "Not catching that bait today."

- "I need a prayer and a snack."

Ask yourself: Is this response a release or a ripple? What do I want the ripple to be?

Shift Happens... But So Can Grace

These moments matter not because God is keeping score, but because they shape *you*. They shape your witness, your home, your heart. What spills out when life squeezes you? That's what's inside. The good news is, you get to fill it with something better. No, you don't need a halo. But you do need awareness, intention, and a few well-timed substitutes that still let you be *you*... just with fewer accidental F-bombs and more laughs.

REFLECTION

What's Your Default Reaction?

This chapter wasn't about being perfect, it was about being prepared. Because let's be honest: the wrong words usually don't sneak out during prayer time or while sipping chamomile tea on the porch. They blast out when life hits us sideways.

So let's pause and reflect:

- What situations most often trip my tongue?

- Do I give myself space to pause, or do I just react?

- Have I tried out a few "clean" go-to phrases so I'm not scrambling in the heat of the moment?

- When I mess up, do I laugh it off and try again — or spiral into shame?

Remember, this isn't about getting it right every time. It's about becoming someone whose heart and mouth reflect peace, presence, and growth. When you react differently than you used to, even just once, that's a win worth celebrating. Let grace keep teaching you. On to the next

BUZ DELIERE

shift.

CHAPTER SEVEN: GRACE FOR THE SLIP-UPS

"The Lord is compassionate and gracious, slow to anger and abounding in faithful love." — *Psalm 103:8*

You ever tell yourself, "I'm going to watch my mouth today," only to end up yelling "SON OF A BAPTIST" before 9:00 a.m.? Maybe it wasn't even a big thing. Maybe it was your dog throwing up on your laptop. Or your toddler finger-painting with peanut butter on your tax documents. Maybe your AirPods vanished into the void again, along with your last ounce of patience. It happens. Not just to new Christians. Not just to the "hotheads." To all of us. No matter how holy your playlist was that morning.

A Real Moment

Here's mine. I was running late, water in one hand, bag in the other, phone wedged between shoulder and ear while answering a work call. I turned the corner too fast and slammed my toe right into the edge of the coffee table. That kind of hit where your brain has a split-second delay before the pain screams through your entire body. And out it came, one of the old faithfuls I've been trying to let go of since my walk with Jesus got real. It didn't feel defiant. It felt automatic. Like years of muscle memory fused into one moment of pain, panic, and poor posture. I've done this so many times, since I was a kid, that I literally have a tattoo on my foot: a little dotted line with scissors, like a cartoon-style surgical suggestion that says, "Yeah, just go ahead and remove this problem area." That toe's been through it. But really, so have I.

That's what hit me harder than the table, how often I'm operating on autopilot. Saying things not because I mean them, but because I've trained myself to react before I even process. That wasn't language from my heart, it was just hardwired habit. Fast, frantic, unfiltered. That one moment didn't make me a failure. But it was a nudge, a holy one, that maybe it's time I stopped sprinting through life barefoot, spiritually speaking. Maybe I need to slow down, reset my patterns, and give the Holy Spirit space to get a word in edgewise. Because sometimes catching it before you shout it doesn't start with silence, it starts with awareness.

The problem isn't just the word that slipped out. It's what's underneath it. That tangle of impatience, pride, stress, fatigue or whatever cocktail of chaos you've been sipping all week. The cuss is often just the foam on top, but instead of beating ourselves up for the bubble, maybe we should check the bottle we've been shaking.

Here's the truth I wish someone had told me earlier. Slipping up doesn't mean you're slipping away. It means you're still in the process. Still human. Still in need of grace and thank God, He gives it in abundance. If we're not careful, though, we turn our little stumbles into spiritual catastrophes. One bad word becomes a bad mood, becomes a bad day, becomes "Well, I guess I'm just bad at this." But that's not how Jesus operates. He didn't come for the already-perfect. He didn't save us so we could earn our keep by never messing up again. He came knowing we'd need mercy on loop. So when you do mess up (and you will), don't go hiding behind guilt or pretending it didn't happen. Call it what it is. Ask for help, and then, this is key, get back up and try again. The goal isn't perfection. It's direction.

Are you headed toward love? Toward patience? Toward self-control? Then you're headed in the right direction, even if you hit a few coffee tables along the way. There's something holy about a heart that doesn't give up. Not because you're stubborn, but because you trust that God's not done with you. And if He's not done with you, you shouldn't be either.

The Difference Between Conviction and Condemnation

There's a big difference between conviction and condemnation, but a lot of us confuse the two, especially when we mess up. Conviction is what the Holy Spirit uses to draw us closer to God. It's like a gentle tap on the shoulder saying, "Hey, that's not who you are anymore." Conviction reminds us that we belong to something better, that we've been called higher. It brings clarity and motivation to change. It inspires hope.

Condemnation, on the other hand, comes from a different place entirely. It shames. It accuses. It isolates. Condemnation whispers, "You'll never change. You'll never be good enough. Why even try?" It doesn't correct, it crushes. I've walked through both. After a slip-up, the voice I hear matters. If that voice sounds like a school principal with a megaphone screaming "SHAME!" That's not Jesus. That's the enemy trying to make me believe my mistake is my identity. Jesus doesn't do that. He didn't look at Peter, the guy who denied Him three times, and say, "You're dead to Me." No, He cooked him breakfast. He restored him. He called him to feed His sheep. We don't serve a God who throws people away when they mess up. We serve a God who kneels down in the dirt, lifts our chin, and says, "Neither do I condemn you. Go and sin no more." (John 8:11)

Notice, He didn't just say "Go." He also said, "Sin no more." Grace doesn't excuse us to keep swearing like sailors in a parking lot showdown. It empowers us to change, even if it's a slow, awkward, two-steps-forward-one-stumble-back kind of change. God's not grading your spiritual growth like a report card. He's walking with you, coaching you, reminding you that your worst moment isn't the final word.

REFLECTION

Grace in Grit

We all drop stuff—pans, phones, and let's be honest, the occasional "holy s#%t." But if the goal here is progress, not perfection, then grace isn't optional, it's essential. Slip-ups will happen. What matters is what you do next.

Take a minute to pause and reflect:

1. What's your usual reaction when you slip up and let something fly?
Do you laugh it off, spiral in guilt, or pretend it didn't happen? Be honest, no halos required.

2. Can you tell the difference between conviction and condemnation in your own life?
Which one shows up more often when you mess up?

3. What would change if you saw your setbacks as reminders of growth, not proof of failure?
Seriously. What if your mess-ups were just part of the map?

4. How might God be inviting you to respond differently next time?
Not with shame but with a deep breath, a pause, and a reset.

5. Bonus: What's your favorite "oops" story so far on this journey?

Because if we can't laugh at ourselves... we'll cry. A lot. Probably in traffic.

CHAPTER EIGHT: RAISING KIDS AND TALKING CLEAN AT HOME

"Train up a child in the way he should go; even when he grows old he will not depart from it."
— Proverbs 22:6

Let's be real for a minute, nothing reminds you how *colorful* your language is like hearing it echoed in a tiny voice from the back seat. "DAD, what's a fudgeknuckle?" "I said *fudgebucket,* buddy. Totally different." If you've got kids—or nieces, nephews, a spouse who sometimes acts like one—you already know, little ears hear *everything,* and little hearts often mimic what they think makes you strong, funny, or "in control." So yeah, this language thing? It's not just about you anymore.

Monkey See, Monkey Shout

One of the wildest things about trying to clean up your language is realizing how deeply your vocabulary has sunk into your home's walls. It's like the baseboards are holding grudges. You drop a spoon and boom, your toddler suddenly becomes a 5'10" longshoreman in a Bluey shirt. Before you start spiraling in parent-guilt, here's the good news, you don't need to raise a bunch of Stepford children who say things like, "Oh dearie me!" when they step on a LEGO. What your kids need most isn't *perfect* language. It's *real* language—with grace, growth, and a sense of humor.

Let me tell you about the time a close friend of mine accidentally dropped an F-bomb in an RV full of Jesus-loving people. We were traveling together, staying in their camper, and they're a solid Christian family, military background, respectful kids, great people. But life in close quarters? That's a different beast. At one point, the mom dropped something on her foot and let it fly, a loud, clear F-bomb that echoed off every surface of that aluminum tube like a spiritual landmine. Then… silence. Then… their 2-year-old son looked up, eyes wide, and just repeated it. Cheerfully. Like he'd just learned the magic password to life. Over, and over, and over while giggling.

We had to shut it down with emergency Bluey. I'm talking a full "here's a tablet, here's a snack, let's pretend that never happened" situation. That moment wasn't about being a "bad Christian." It was just a real moment. A human one. A reminder that little ears don't wait for perfect circumstances to copy what they hear. Kids repeat what feels powerful, even if it's not what we meant to teach them. That's why what we model matters. Even when we slip, how we respond to the slip is part of the lesson too.

From Curse Words to Catchphrases

Some families have what I call "Legacy Language." Maybe your dad said "Son of a monkey wrench!" every time the car wouldn't start. Maybe Grandma's go-to was "Lord help my liver." These phrases stick, not because they were fancy, but because they were *theirs.* You get to create that for your home. Start by swapping some of your go-to outbursts with new ones that feel *genuine,* not forced. The more often you use them, the more likely they'll stick, for you and your little mimics. It's not about making your house a censorship zone. It's about making your voice something worth repeating.

Modeling the Shift

You don't need a whiteboard and a family seminar on "language improvement." Just start living it. When you mess up, call it out with humility. "Whew, that word wasn't my best. Let me try again." Let your kids see that even adults are still learning how to handle frustration without blowing a gasket. That lesson? Way more powerful than pretending to never slip. Also, don't underestimate the power of a funny replacement. Your kid may not remember your lecture on kindness, but they *will* remember when you dropped a jar of salsa and shouted, "Cheese and rice on a cracker!"

What About Spouses, Roommates, or Reluctant Teens?

Maybe you're the only one in your house even *trying* to shift your words. That's okay. You're not the language police. You're just setting a new tone. People might roll their eyes at first but give it time. Consistency is contagious. Try using humor to bring them in. "Hey, instead of swearing, wanna try calling it a 'blasted butt-nugget' next time?" They'll laugh. You'll all feel a little lighter. Mission accomplished.

What If You're in a Blended Family or the Only One Shifting?

Maybe you're trying to make this Holy Shift, but your spouse isn't. Or your co-parent rolls their eyes when you say "crud muffins." Or maybe your teenage stepkid calls your clean speech "cringe" and still swears like they've got a secret side hustle as a pirate. Breathe. You're not the language cop. You're just setting the tone. You don't need to nag or lecture or correct everyone else's mouth. What works better? Keep modeling the kind of language that reflects who *you* are becoming and let the fruit speak for itself.

Here are a few quiet wins that plant seeds without pushing:

- Use humor instead of guilt: "That word's above my pay grade now. I'm down to yelling about casseroles."

- Let your replacement phrases become a running family joke. If your kids roll their eyes when you say

"Pickle juice!", good. They're paying attention.

- Celebrate *progress*, not perfection. Even if someone else only swaps out one word… that's still a shift.

You don't need everyone on the same page to start writing a new chapter. Just be faithful on your line. Your words will echo longer than you think.

REFLECTION

Keep It Honest at Home

Your language is planting seeds—everywhere you go, but especially at home. Whether you're raising babies, bonding with teens, or doing life with adults who still throw tantrums over Tupperware lids, your words matter.

1. What language do you remember hearing growing up?
What stuck with you and what do you want to do differently?

2. How do you react when your child or someone in your home swears?
Do you correct, connect, or combust?

3. What's one silly, memorable phrase you could start using instead of a swear word?
(Make it weird. Those are the best ones.)

4. How can you lead by example without being preachy?
Think in terms of tone, grace, and consistency.

5. Who in your home could use a little more encouragement when they mess up?
(Yes, it might be you.)

Think about this..

"What phrases are your kids likely to remember from you 10 years from now?"

"When your child is angry or stressed, what kind of vocabulary do you want them to default to, and where will they learn it?"

CHAPTER NINE: HOW TO BE CLEAN WITHOUT BEING CRINGE

"Let the righteous one strike me—it is an act of faithful love; let him rebuke me—it is oil for my head; let me not refuse it." —Psalm 141:5

So… you've swapped out the four-letter bombs for "fudge nuggets" and "shut the front door." Good job. You're doing it. Now you've got this sneaking suspicion that people are looking at you like you just stepped out of a PBS puppet show. You're trying to speak life but what's coming out sounds like Ned Flanders had a baby with a camp counselor and they named it "Hokey McGee." Welcome to the awkward teenage years of clean talk. This is the part nobody warns you about. You clean up your mouth, but suddenly your words feel like they're wearing a costume. You're in this weird in-between where "real you" is still under construction, but "church you" sounds like they just got off the phone with their accountability partner.

And worst of all? You're worried you're losing your edge.

I've been there. Picture it: I'm in the middle of a high-stress lunch rush in the kitchen, three tickets deep, a fryer smoking like it's reenacting Mount Sinai. A server walks in and says, "Hey, the vegan customer wants to know if the chicken stock in the soup is cruelty-free."

I pause. I take a breath. I want to say things that would make the walls weep. Instead, I say… "Bless my brisket. That's a new one." The room goes silent. One cook raises an eyebrow. Another stifles a laugh. I suddenly feel like I just auditioned for the role of "Youth Pastor Who Tries Too Hard" in a local skit. Here's what I've learned the hard way: **authenticity isn't about being edgy, it's about being real.** Real with your words. Real with your heart. Real with your people. Clean speech isn't supposed to be fake, it's supposed to be true. So if "shucks-a-rooni" makes you sound like an off-brand cartoon character? Ditch it. Find words that fit your personality, not someone else's Pinterest board. Let's be honest, some alternatives are just... bad. No one wants to sound like a Christian AI trying to pass the Turing Test. The goal isn't to replace swear words with squeaky toys. It's to develop a language that reflects who you are, who you're becoming, and the God who's helping you get there. You don't have to choose between being funny and being faithful. You don't have to lose your style to find your sanctification. You can still be salty, just seasoned—like the verse says. Flavorful, not foul.

Let's break down a few ways to clean it up without cringing yourself into oblivion:

1. Ditch the Overly Churchy Clichés

Not every clean phrase needs to sound like it was sponsored by Hobby Lobby. I once heard a guy stub his toe and shout, "Great googly Moses on a mountaintop!" He froze immediately after, like he wasn't sure if he had just worshiped or blasphemed. No one knew how to respond. Do we laugh? Do we pray? Is this a revival?

Clean language doesn't need to be weird. It just needs to be *you*. Don't try to channel a 1920s cartoon if that's not your vibe.

2. Keep Your Delivery Natural

A friend of mine tried to replace all his cussing with the word "zucchini." That was his go-to. Anytime something went wrong — spilled drink, traffic, jammed finger — he'd shout, "ZUCCHINI!" At first, it was kind of funny, but then it got weird. Like, emotionally unhinged weird. Hearing someone growl "ZUCCHINI!!!" in a moment of rage makes you feel like you accidentally joined a cult that worships farmer's markets.

The problem wasn't the word. It was the delivery. Clean words spoken in the same tone as a demon summon don't make you sound holy, they just make you sound haunted.

3. Laugh at Yourself

I once tried to sub in "Oh biscuits and gravy!" during a kitchen rush. I was under pressure, sweating, burned my hand and that phrase just fell out of my mouth like a broken shelf. The line cook next to me didn't say anything. He just slowly turned, handed me the tongs, and said, "Bro, I'm gonna need you to never say that again." We both laughed. It broke the tension, and later, *he* started saying "bless it" when things went sideways.

Turns out, awkward clean talk can be contagious, in the best way.

4. Know Your Audience

You don't need to give the same performance in every room. You can be more relaxed at home and a little more filtered in front of your grandma, that's not two-faced, that's just wisdom. I once heard a guy try to clean up his language during a men's Bible study. He normally swore like a mechanic with a hangover, but that night he swapped every curse with the word "hugs." I mean *every one*. "I don't give a flying HUG what that guy thinks." "That was a bunch of HUGGING nonsense." "Then my boss came in and tried to HUG me over!" It... did not land.

We all sat there like: Is he threatening people with affection? Is this a cry for help? Eventually, he just gave up and said, "Sorry, y'all. I'm still under construction." Honestly? That moment was better than all the weird word-swapping, because it was *honest*.

5. Don't Try So Hard

You don't have to sound like a Christian meme account to be clean. One woman I know tried to switch her usual curse word with "hallelujah" but only during road rage. Let me tell you something: if you scream "HALLELUJAH!" while cutting someone off in traffic, it does not come across as spirit-filled. It feels like you're casting a holy hex at 65 mph. The goal isn't to be dramatic. It's to be intentional. Keep it human. Keep it honest.

6. Season, Don't Sugarcoat

Jesus didn't say, "You are the vanilla pudding of the earth." He said *salt*. That means speak with flavor, not fluff. Here's the difference, sugarcoating says what's easy. Seasoning says what's needed, but in a way people can actually hear it. You don't have to douse everything in honey but you also don't need to light people up like you're on a roast battle with Satan. Clean language doesn't mean soft language. It means **intentional** language. Precise. Purposeful. Seasoned.

I had a friend who cleaned up his language but lost all his fire. He'd start saying things like, "Well... if it's not too much trouble... perhaps we could consider... maybe... just a thought..."
I finally told him, "You sound like you're asking someone to prom, not leading a meeting." He wasn't speaking with salt. He was using Splenda. You can still be bold and clean. You can still correct someone without sounding like you're apologizing for existing. You don't have to yell to be heard, but you do need to speak in a way that leaves a mark, not a scar. The best flavor? Grace, with a little bite. Like when Jesus told the woman at the well, "Go and sin no more." He

didn't shame her. He seasoned her life with truth that still set her free. Your words don't need to sound safe. They need to sound *real*. Clean speech isn't about avoiding conflict, it's about speaking with such intentional seasoning that it actually sinks in.

What If You're the Funny One?

Let's talk to my sarcasm squad, class clowns, and roastmasters for a second. Sometimes, when you're known for being "the funny one," cleaning up your speech can feel like getting a personality transplant. You're afraid of losing your edge. You don't want to sound like a spiritual Stepford wife. Here's what I've learned, **you don't need cussing to be funny, you just need timing and truth.**

Clean humor done well is actually *funnier*, because it's unexpected. It catches people off guard without catching them in the throat. It punches up, not down. And it lasts longer than a cheap shock laugh. Some of the funniest people I know never swear. They just see the world sideways and describe it with accuracy, wit, and just enough sass to keep it spicy. You can be sharp without being harsh. Sarcastic without being mean. Honest without being hurtful. That's the kind of funny that stays with people and earns you real respect.

Final Thoughts from the Fryer

Language is more than letters, it's lifestyle. It reflects what's going on inside. And while this journey to cleaner speech might feel awkward at times, it's worth it. Because the point isn't to sound perfect. It's to speak with purpose.

And that? That'll never be cringe.

REFLECTION:

Salt & Sound

Let's be honest, there's a fine line between sounding clean and sounding like you were homeschooled by a VeggieTales DVD. The fear of coming off as cheesy, fake, or like you're trying *way too hard* is real. But here's the thing: you're not trying to become someone else. You're trying to become more of *you*, just with less debris flying out of your mouth when you're under stress. This chapter was all about keeping it real while cleaning it up. Not ditching your edge, just sharpening it with grace. So before we move on to the final shift, take a beat and think through what authenticity looks and sounds like for *you*.

1. What's a "clean phrase" you've tried that felt super unnatural?
Did you ditch it or tweak it to make it feel more *you*? It's okay if "cheese and crackers!" didn't exactly roll off the tongue.

2. Are you afraid of sounding fake if you stop swearing?
What would it look like to stay authentic *and* intentional with your words?

3. Think of someone you know who speaks cleanly but still sounds real.

What makes their tone or delivery work? How can you borrow some of that style without copying it?

4. This week, notice how you sound when you're under pressure.
When things go sideways—your coffee spills, your kid repeats you at church, your flight gets delayed, how do you respond?
What would it look like to *season* those moments with grace *and* personality?

"What's the most awkward clean phrase you've used so far?"

"Who's someone in your life that speaks kindly but still sounds like themselves, what can you learn from them?"

CHAPTER TEN: BECAUSE GROWTH DOESN'T ALWAYS SOUND POLISHED

"Above all else, guard your heart, for everything you do flows from it."
— Proverbs 4:23

If you've made it to the end of this book, then you're

probably not just someone who "drops stuff." You're someone who wants to grow. You're someone who has felt the tension of wanting to honor God with your mouth without sounding like a corny caricature of yourself. You don't want to trade personality for perfection or authenticity for a script. You just want your words to line up with who you're becoming and if possible, still sound like a functioning adult who occasionally uses sarcasm, humor, and emotion without needing to apologize to the entire congregation.

This book was never about legalism. It wasn't about scrubbing your vocabulary so clean that you lose your voice in the process. It was about recognizing how powerful your words are. It was about learning to pause long enough to notice what's driving your reactions, and about realizing that some of those old habits don't reflect the person you're becoming.

Along the way, you've picked up some new tools. You've learned why your words matter, how they carry weight and influence not just in the spiritual world, but in the everyday moments of work, home, and relationships. You've practiced how to pause, how to catch the moment before it explodes, and how to swap in something better when it feels like your filter is on fire. And maybe, just maybe, you've started to feel the difference between talking like your old self and speaking like someone who's being shaped by grace.

Let's be clear, this is not the finish line. It's more like a rest stop on the way to something bigger. You're going to slip. You'll still say something questionable when your kid drops your phone in the toilet, or when the line at the DMV moves at the speed of anointing oil. You may even invent a brand-new phrase that confuses your pastor and makes your grandma reach for her Bible.

And that's okay.

The point of this process was never to arrive at perfection. The goal is presence. It's being aware of what you say, who's listening, and what it's saying about your heart. This isn't about pretending to be holy. It's about becoming more whole.

Each time you pause and choose your words on purpose, you're building a new habit. Those moments, though small, begin to add up. One clean phrase here. One less blowup there. One moment where you bite your tongue and breathe instead of blast. Those aren't just wins; they're proof that you're changing.

Here's something you may not realize yet, this shift isn't just for you. It's for the people around you too. Every time you choose kindness over sarcasm, or patience over profanity, you're planting seeds. You're showing your kids, your coworkers, your friends—even the guy in line at the gas station—that your voice doesn't have to be loud or laced with venom to be strong. You're creating a new kind of influence, one that doesn't demand attention, but earns respect.

You may never know the full impact of your words, but someone else will. It might be your child listening from the backseat, your spouse watching how you handle stress, or a stranger who just needed a little grace that day. You won't always get credit for it, and that's not the point. God sees it. He honors it, and He's working through it, even when it doesn't feel like much.

Learning to clean up your language isn't about being impressive. It's about being aligned. When your words reflect the work God is doing in your heart, even the smallest conversation can carry significance. Even the silly substitutions you've picked up, those holy placeholders, can become reminders of progress.

So, don't stop now. Keep practicing. Keep pausing. Keep laughing at the slip-ups and celebrating the wins. You're not failing because you still mess up; you're growing because you care enough to notice and try again.

This isn't about sounding "Christian." It's about sounding like someone who's being changed—slowly, steadily, and with a whole lot of grace.

You've made a holy shift. Now walk in it.

REFLECTION:

Guard & Give Grace

1. Think back to when you first picked up this book. How did you feel about your language at the time—proud, frustrated, indifferent?

2. What's one recent moment where you caught yourself before cursing—or swapped in a cleaner phrase that felt natural? Celebrate it. That counts.

3. What's still tough? Is it certain people, certain situations, or trying to be funny under pressure?

4. How have you grown—not just in what you say, but in how you think before you speak?

5. If your words are a window to your heart, what do you hope people see when you speak?

A NOTE FROM THE AUTHOR

Hey there,

If nobody's told you lately, I'm proud of you. Not because you're perfect (you're not), but because you showed up. You read a book that leaned into honesty, humor, faith, and probably made you laugh out loud at least once during a traffic jam or bathroom break. This wasn't just about "watching your language." It was about watching your life and asking: Do my words line up with the person I'm becoming? I didn't write this because I've mastered it. I wrote it because I've lived it. Cursed under my breath in church parking lots. Dropped "oh ship" in the kitchen and meant something entirely different, and still, God didn't quit on me. So I won't quit on me either, and I hope you won't quit on you. You've got what it takes to make this shift. Not because you're strong but because grace is. Not because you're fake but because you're learning. One holy word at a time.

Keep going. I'm rooting for you.

—Buz Deliere
Chef, writer, fellow language reformer, grace addict

FINAL PRAYER

A Shifted Heart, A Steady Voice

God,
Thank You for not giving up on me, even when my mouth gets ahead of my mind. Thank You for grace that covers my slip-ups and strength that helps me grow.

Help me pause when I want to react. Help me speak life when I feel frustration. Help me shift my language not to impress others, but to reflect You. Give me words that build, not break. That comfort, not cut. That bring joy, not just jokes.

Remind me that change is a process, not a performance. And let every awkward "shizzle" and "fudge bucket" be a reminder I'm choosing a new way. One holy shift at a time. It's in Jesus' name we pray,

Amen.

THE HOLY SHIFT FIELD MANUAL (QUICK RECAP EDITION)

So... you made it. You've dropped stuff, dropped some spicy words, picked up a few "crud muffins," and hopefully picked up some peace along the way.

In case your brain is as overloaded as your junk drawer, here's a lightning-fast recap for your road ahead:

It's not about legalism. It's about alignment.

You don't have to sound like Ned Flanders. Just sound like a growing version of you.

Your kids will say what you say. Make it something worth repeating.

Grace is real. Shame is a liar.

If you yell "Sweet mother of meatballs!" in traffic, you're

doing it right.

God's not counting your slip-ups. He's helping you catch them.

One Holy Shift at a time… is still a Holy Shift.

Keep it weird. Keep it real. Keep it holy-ish.

You've got this.

ACKNOWLEDGEMENT

To the ones who heard me cuss before they heard me pray, thank you for sticking around.

To my family and friends who've endured years of hot pans, loud words, and unfinished sentences, y'all are the real MVPs. Thanks for loving me through the shifts and not flinching when I yelled, "Mother of pearl!" like I meant it.

To my church fam, especially the ones who knew me before the vocabulary upgrade, your grace made room for growth. Thanks for never confusing my mouth with my heart.

To the chefs, athletes, bounty hunters, kitchen crews, coaches, and coworkers who taught me how to speak fire under pressure, and to the Holy Spirit who taught me how to cool it down, this book is for all of us.

To my readers — the real ones, the recovering hotheads, the "Jesus-loving but still dropping stuff" crew — you're not alone. Thanks for walking this awkward, hilarious, holy journey with me. I hope you found something in these pages that made you laugh, think, pause, or pray.

To my early readers, and anyone who told me "This is actually helpful," you helped bring this thing to life. You caught typos, tightened tangents, and kept the voice real. You made me sound smarter (and cleaner) than I probably am.

And to Jesus, the only one who can truly clean a heart, rewire a reflex, and make something holy out of a hot mess. Thank You for never giving up on my mouth… or the rest of me.

Let's keep making a Holy Shift.

Made in the USA
Coppell, TX
02 February 2026